Instant Readers™
Teacher's Guide

Developed with

Bernice E. Cullinan

Roger C. Farr

Barbara Peterson

Nancy Roser

Dorothy S. Strickland

Harcourt

Orlando   Boston   Dallas   Chicago   San Diego
Visit *The Learning Site!*
www.harcourtschool.com

CONTENTS

"What can I do to MEET THE NEEDS of the *emerging readers* in my classroom?"

Instant Readers Offer Instructional Choices and Help

by Dr. Dorothy S. Strickland and Dr. Bernice E. Cullinan

Dr. Strickland is the State of New Jersey Professor of Reading at Rutgers University in New Brunswick, New Jersey.
Dr. Cullinan is a Professor of Reading at New York University in New York City.

School dismissal time, mid-February: Maria pauses in the midst of the end-of-school-day hubbub as her first graders prepare to go home. She smiles as she notes how much independence the children have gained in packing their backpacks and pulling on their boots as they prepare to face the challenge of the rainstorm outside. Most of all, however, she is thrilled with the knowledge that they are all steadily gaining independence in literacy.

Last September, she would never have believed this would be true of several youngsters in this group. She could remember thinking, "I have never seen such a diverse group. Mario, Joline, and Harry were readers when they entered kindergarten. Marcia, Hernando, Julia, and Darryl barely know a few letters of the alphabet. Everyone else is at various points in between. This is going to be an impossible year."

As always, it was the children at the ends of the spectrum that troubled her most. But those at the lower end had always been the most baffling. In the past, she had complained that they were the children who seemed to "slip through the cracks." Instinctively, she knew that they needed more instructional time with her than she could manage to give them; perhaps some different materials might help as well. But most of all, she knew that she was lacking in the "know-how" required to pull it all together.

Sharing her concerns with Lynn, another first-grade teacher, Maria learned about some workshops given by a trained Reading Recovery teacher on "Reading Recovery Strategies for the Classroom." It was there that Maria and Lynn gained a better understanding of the reading process, learned about the use of little books, and practiced doing running records to assess student learning and making instructional decisions based on what they learned.

After the workshops were over, Maria and Lynn continued to read, discuss, and try out new intervention strategies. Moreover, they were actively using little books for varied purposes with all of their students and getting better and better results.

The Harcourt Brace *Instant Readers* are based on the research foundations and philosophical beliefs that Lynn and Maria used as they redefined their first-grade programs (Clay, 1985). The *Instant Readers* series makes it possible for them to develop a balanced instructional program with components found to be included in successful early intervention programs (Wong, Groth, and O'Flahavan, 1995).

CONTINUOUS ASSESSMENT

Teachers help students select texts at the right challenge level and use a variety of informal tools to assess reading ability.

The *Instant Readers* series
- helps struggling readers experience success and gain confidence.
- helps better readers build fluency and develop competence.
- provides teachers with guidance in the use of running records and other informal assessment tools.

VARIED GROUPING FORMATS

Reading is taught in the context of a variety of formats and for a variety of purposes.

The *Instant Readers* series
- is designed to be used within the context of flexible grouping, combining whole-group with small-group instruction.
- employs reading for a variety of purposes, such as for guided reading, shared reading, buddy reading, and readers' circles.

The chart in Figure 1 offers some possibilities for planning and organizing reading and writing instruction with *Instant Readers*. Opportunities for varied instructional activities and purposes are given in a three-stage reading/language arts time period.

Figure 1
Organizing Reading and Writing Instruction Time with *Instant Readers*

GROUPING FORMATS	INSTRUCTIONAL ACTIVITIES	PURPOSES
Whole-Group	Reading Aloud, Shared Reading and Writing, and Guided Reading	Strategy Lessons: comprehension, responses to literature, reading and writing, follow-up activities to previous whole-group session, determine small-group and individual instruction based on whole-group observations
Planning Time: Brief time prior to Workshop Activities where children discuss who goes where, what they do, and when.		
Small-Group and Individual	Rereading activities such as buddy reading, listening center reading, small-group instruction in *Instant Readers* or other materials, writing and reading conferences, center-based activities, and ongoing assessment	Strategy Lessons: word recognition, follow-up activities from whole-group or previous small-group sessions, running records

EMBEDDED WORD STUDY

All students are actively engaged in a variety of word study activities.

The *Instant Readers* series
- balances meaning and word study by focusing first readings on comprehension and interpretation and subsequent readings on close analysis of textual features.
- includes word study strategies of phonemic awareness, phonics, and structural analysis.
- includes the full range of cueing systems sound/letter relationships, word meaning, and sentence structure.
- includes activities that take students beyond the text to further word study, such as the study of word families, and to the application of these activities to writing.

Little books lead to reading success because they

- have predictable language in patterned phrases and sentences,
- give visual clues in colorful, engaging illustrations,
- tell a good story and give interesting information,
- relate experiences children understand, and
- combine controlled text with creative storytelling.

A home-school program is ongoing and organized as an integral part of instruction. Extending the learning to at-home activities is a key part of the *Instant Readers* series.

The *Instant Readers* series
- includes activities for at-home support.
- includes a monitoring process for parents, teachers, and children to keep track of at-home reading.

For example, when children successfully complete a variety of activities with an *Instant Reader* at school, the book is taken home to be shared with a reading buddy. The book might be placed in a plastic bag with a form such as the "Buddy Reading at Home" form (see Figure 2). When the book and form are returned, the child notes this on the "Reading Buddy Log" (see Figure 3).

Figure 2

Buddy Reading at Home

TO: At-Home Reading Buddy

FROM: ___________ (teacher's name) ___________

Please read the enclosed book with your reading buddy. Do at least one activity, fill out the form, and return it tomorrow. Thank you.

(Name of child)_________________________________ and I read

(Name of book)_________________________________ together.

We also (briefly tell what else you did)

____

____

Below are some suggested activities that can be done with any book:

- Discuss the story.
- Draw a picture to go with the book.
- Write another story like this one.
- Act out parts of the story.
- Read the story again with another reading buddy.
- Tape-record a second reading.
- Make a puppet of one of the story characters.
- Write about a favorite part of the story.

_________________________________ Date ___________________

(signed by Reading Buddy)

BOOKS	NAME
	Jordan
[TEACHER: List names of all the books in order of difficulty. Then copy sheets and place in three-ring binder or portfolio for individual children.]	[When book and form are returned, child writes name next to book's title to show that the book has been read.]
My Dog	JORDAh
What a Shower!	JORDAn
Spring Pops Up	
All Fall Down	

Teachers like Maria and Lynn know they will always have students who differ greatly in their instruction needs. They are aware that students need to practice reading often to become fluent readers. The engaging stories of the *Instant Readers* series, varied grouping and instructional activities at school, plus buddy reading at home make a combination that works.

Guidelines for Choosing Texts for Beginning Readers

by Dr. Barbara Peterson

For her doctoral dissertation, Dr. Peterson examined characteristics of texts used in the Reading Recovery® program and developed a rubric to guide teachers in arranging texts along a gradient of difficulty. She continues to examine text levels and text characteristics essential for emerging readers' development.

One of the most challenging tasks for a teacher of beginning readers is selecting books that will support a reader's current instructional needs. A text that looks easy on the surface because it contains few words or uses repeated sentence patterns may be too difficult for a reader, while a longer text with some unusual vocabulary might be a perfect match. The purpose of this article is to provide guidelines to help teachers evaluate and arrange texts in an approximate order of difficulty. First, bear in mind the following needs and objectives.

About Readers

- Readers need to read every day, many times a day.
- Readers need a supply of easy, familiar books they can read (and reread) independently, with phrasing and fluency.
- Readers need books appropriate for their instructional level (a text read with an accuracy level of 90 – 95% is usually considered instructionally appropriate for a particular student).
- Readers need to hear stories read aloud that are too difficult for them to read independently.
- Readers can also read more difficult material by working collaboratively with a more proficient reader.

About Teachers

- A teacher's knowledge of a text and a student is more important than the level of the text.
- The teacher, not the text, is the agent of change in reading acquisition.
- Teachers will fail their students if they consider only a text level when selecting a book for a reader.
- According to Marie Clay, the focal issue is "What kind of teacher-child interaction accompanies the reading?" (Clay, 1991b)

> **H**ow do I **choose** the *right* **books** for emerging readers?

Developing a List of Benchmark Books

- Teachers should work together to pool their knowledge and experience about the texts currently in use in their school. There is no formula suitable for leveling books for beginning readers.
- Select 15 or 20 texts (different instructional levels) that most children seem to like and read successfully ("little books," selections from reading texts and children's literature).
- Arrange these texts in order from easiest to most difficult.
- Discuss this list; add other texts to fill in gaps; remove texts if others are found to be more suitable.
- Use this "Benchmark List" as a framework for evaluating and leveling other texts, including the Harcourt Brace *Instant Readers*.
- Benchmark books may also be used as touchstones for marking reading progress for individual children.
- It is not necessary to use a particular leveling system; find what works best for your school.

About Levels

- A book level is only an *approximate* indicator of difficulty.
- A new level may be assigned to a book if teachers agree it belongs at another level.
- Levels *assist* teachers in book selection.
- Children do *not* read all books at each level.

The most extensive information about texts and beginning readers has come from the Reading Recovery® program, where books are organized into a gradient of 20 levels. Texts at levels 1 and 2 consist of simple stories or descriptions of events familiar to young children, while books at levels 19 and 20 contain well-developed stories typical of those found at the end of first-grade reading programs. (See the chart on the following page.)

Within each level, there are many variations in style. Consequently, it is not possible to precisely describe the characteristics at each level. Broad shifts along a gradient of difficulty can be described, however. Assigning a level to a book is a process of taking into account various features of texts, including *content, illustrations, vocabulary, repetition of language patterns, language structures, narrative structure,* and *text layout*.

The following chart provides a framework for showing some of the changes that occur between groups of levels. It is recommended that classroom teachers and Reading Recovery® teachers work closely together to create a leveled booklist to support the classroom instructional program of their school.

Profiles of Books for Beginning Readers

Levels 1-4 consistent placement of print
repetition of 1-2 sentence patterns (1-2 word changes)
oral language structures
familiar objects and actions
illustrations provide high support for the printed message

Levels 5-8 repetition of 2-3 sentence patterns (phrases may change)
opening, closing sentences vary
   or varied simple sentence patterns
oral language structures predominate, with a gradual
   introduction of written language structures
many familiar objects and actions
illustrations provide moderate–high support

Levels 9-12 repetition of 3 or more sentence patterns
   or varied sentence patterns (repeated phrases or refrains)
blend of oral and written language structures
topics include familiar experiences and imaginative events
illustrations provide moderate support

Levels 13-15 varied sentence patterns (may have repeated
   phrases or refrains)
   or repeated patterns in cumulative form
written language structures
oral structures appear in dialogue
conventional story; literary language
specialized vocabulary for some topics
illustrations provide low–moderate support

Levels 16-20 elaborated episodes and events
extended descriptions
links to familiar stories
literary language
unusual, challenging vocabulary
illustrations provide low support

© Barbara Peterson. *Characteristics of Texts that Support Beginning Readers.*
Unpublished doctoral dissertation. The Ohio State University. 1988.

"WHAT MAKES A GOOD BOOK INTRODUCTION—ESPECIALLY WHEN THE BOOK IS SO SHORT?"

Take Longer than an "Instant": Introducing Children to Instant Readers

by Dr. Nancy Roser

Dr. Roser is a Professor of Language and Literacy Studies at the University of Texas, Austin.

When you introduce two of your friends who haven't yet met one another, you understand that a successful introduction depends upon your knowing what your two friends have in common, as well as something uniquely interesting about each. You want to say something intriguing enough about each friend so the chat that follows your introduction has a smooth beginning. Once begun, the interaction of the two new acquaintances may open topics and uncover shared interests that you (who know them both) didn't anticipate.

Similarly, when children encounter a book for the first time—one they will read and return to—they often require such a planned introduction. Similar to bringing two friends together, successful introductions depend upon knowing both parties well enough to find a likely common link. The best introductions to new stories for young readers provide a "peek" at the story, invite connections, encourage speculation/ prediction, and even get some of the story language rolling about on the tongue—all without giving away the essence. Quite a task.

PREPARING THE BOOK INTRODUCTION

Even when a text is "predictable" in terms of its language (repetitive, rhythmic, rhyming), its surface simplicity may offer themes that stretch or topics that require exploration. Teachers who offer introductions to stories ensure that the content, concepts, and word choices are accessible to children. They can identify potential trouble spots and work them into the introduction.

Daniel, a first-grade teacher, takes time to read any new book carefully (and at least twice) before introducing it to his children. He reports that his procedure is to read slowly and *attend to his own thoughts* as he reads. His sensitivity to his own initial reactions makes him a spontaneous, open discussion partner later. While preparing an introduction to the Harcourt Brace *Instant Reader* titled *A Place for Nicholas*, he described his steps like this:

1) I read the story the first time to decide what it meant to me and what it would likely mean to the children. For example, Nicholas's need for a "place" reminded me of my own clumsy attempts as a child to build backyard tents and closet corners and even to pull the tablecloth low enough to make a hideout under the dining table. The adult theme of Virginia Woolf's *A Room of One's Own* even occurred to me and convinced me that Nicholas's need for a private space is universal. I decided to use that need for place to open the discussion—and encourage my children to describe the meanings they attach to that need and the ways they satisfy it.

2) I read again to pay close attention to the story language, which parts of it recurred and were manageable and which parts seemed unlikely to be decoded or even understood. I decided to use Nicholas's name repeatedly as we talked about the story, as well as to drop the names of his brother and sister into the conversation. I wanted to make sure I used the repeated phrases "his own place" during the introduction so that the story language *and* problem would seem familiar.

3) I then looked carefully at the illustrations in preparation for the "picture walk" that we would take as a way of introducing the story. There were several things I noted—that almost all of the family was "busy" except for Nicholas—Mom at her computer, Jeff with his toys, and Kelly helping Dad. I noticed the backyard tree that would have made a wonderful treehouse "place" for me as a boy. I noticed that Nicholas had books, toys, paintings, a dog, and siblings, and I wondered why he wasn't as busy as the rest of his family. I noted how resourceful his younger brother was in solving the problem; I watched the range of expressions on the dog's face. Certainly, within an eight-page book, there was a great deal to see, to think about, and, depending on my children's leads, to talk about.

Taking a "Picture Walk"

Daniel used a "picture walk" as a way of introducing his young readers to the structure, concepts, and language patterns of *A Place for Nicholas*. By guiding the children as a museum curator might, he helped to focus the task, pique interest, and support the reading to come. He planned support in the forms of using key story words, encouraging curious speculation about the pictured events, and asking for evidence for interpretations. Listen in on Daniel's class as he leads a picture walk with a small group:

Daniel: (opening the cover wide so that front and back show) Let's look at a new book. The title is *A Place for Nicholas*. It was written by Lucy Floyd and illustrated by David McPhail. What seems to be going on here?

Adam: A family working.

Beth: Those two aren't workin'!

Carl: That one's playing. Is that a boy? He isn't doing *anything*.

Debra: My mom works on a computer.

Daniel: The story is called *A Place for Nicholas*. Who do you think Nicholas may be?

Ernie: The dog. There's a doghouse.

Beth: Maybe that sad boy because there's no place for him to work.

Carl: I think he wants to use the mower, but his sister won't let him.

Debra: Maybe he wants to play on the computer…

Adam: …or that might be his airplane and his brother won't share. My brother won't share.

Daniel: Debra said the boy on the steps looked sad. How can you tell?

Debra: His mouth goes down, and his eyes go [demonstrates] and he's grumpy.

Carl: He's probably Nicholas.

Adam: That's his only place—the steps.

Daniel: You think this is Nicholas and there is no place for him?

Several: Yeah. Yep.

Daniel: [turns to the title page and says nothing but just shows the picture]

Beth: He's got his eyes open.

Ernie: His dog feels sorry.

Daniel: What makes you think so?

Ernie: He got his face up like this [demonstrates].

Adam: My dog bumps his head on me when I'm mad.

Debra: Is *that* Nicholas?

Daniel: Yes, the boy is Nicholas, and the story is called…

Several: *A Place for Nicholas.*

Carl: Because Nicholas don't have no place.

Daniel: What do you mean, Carl?

Carl: He only has to sit on the steps.

Beth: Maybe he was bad.

Daniel: Let's see (turns to page 2 and shows only one picture). Nicholas doesn't seem to have a place here.

Debra: Uh huh. His mother's playing with the little boy.

Daniel: Yes, his brother, Jeff.

Ernie: She's not playin'.

Carl: He got to come inside.

Beth: But he's not happy.

Daniel: Nicholas seems to need a place, doesn't he? [turns to page 3, on which Nicholas's dad gestures toward the house]

Adam: His dad thinks he should play upstairs.

Beth: That sister's not busy.

Daniel: His sister Kelly has stopped mowing, hasn't she?

Carl: If I was him, I'd use that mower.

Daniel: I think this tree would make a nice place. He could have it all for himself. I made a treehouse when I was a boy.

Debra: It looks too high; he's little.

Ernie: Yeah, he's only about four because he wears those baby clothes.

Daniel: Nicholas must need a place of his own.

Beth: Without all the people. Like in my family at Christmas.

Daniel: People all around can make you feel like finding a place of your own [turning to page 4, where Kelly swings Jeff].

Adam: They won't give him a turn.

Debra: He's pouting.

Carl: She's probably saying, "Go in the house. We're all outside now. Then you can have a place."

Ernie: I have a place under the steps. It has brooms. It's my office.

Daniel: Ernie has a place with nobody but him. [turning to page 5 in the bedroom] But as for Nicholas...

Debra: He has to share with his *brother*.

Several: Me, too! Me, too! I do, too. Not my brother, my sister.

Daniel: [shows pages six and seven] Now what?

Adam: He says, "never mind."

Beth: [as Nicholas] "I'm gettin' out of here."

Carl: They're gonna make a tent.

Daniel: How do you know?

Ernie: We did that! We did it outside between trees. We put a blanket over a rope. A tent!

Debra: The dog doesn't want them to.

Ernie: Uh huh. He's helping.

Daniel: Helping Jeff?

Adam: I think I know what the place is.

Beth: For Nicholas.

Daniel: [turning to page 8] His very own place?

Adam: What'd they tie that to on this side?

Debra: I think he got what he wanted.

Ernie: One time, when my brother and me wanted to build a place in our room...

Daniel has secured the beginning of a link between two friends—a group of eager students and a story that taps a universal theme. His students have focused, speculated, detoured, and elaborated. Their upcoming reading has been supported. A picture walk can be longer or shorter than this transcript. Depending upon the "scaffolding" the young readers need, the concepts, words, characters, problems, or language patterns of the text can be previewed. All of this can smooth the initial reading.

Book introductions and picture walks are ways of turning acquaintances into friends. It takes longer than an instant, but the effects on thought, talk, connection, and successful reading last even longer.

Monitoring Individual Progress with *Instant Readers*

by Dr. Roger C. Farr

Dr. Farr is the Chancellors' Professor of Education and the Director of the Center for Reading and Language Studies at Indiana University in Bloomington.

The most useful information you can collect about your children's reading is the information you gather as part of regular instruction and during the reading of texts. This kind of assessment provides information about how children actually read text and what they do during class time. Running records, along with kidwatching and anecdotal records, are the three common methods for engaging in this kind of informal assessment.

RUNNING RECORDS

A running record is a procedure you can use to learn about a child's oral reading. (Clay, 1993) The goal is to learn as much as you can about the child's reading strategies. While the student is reading aloud, you record everything that he or she says or does.

The best approach is to have a student choose a selection that he or she would *like* to read. Use the form on page 19 to help you record the reading. Running records are usually based on a student's reading of 100 to 200 words. On a copy of the selection, mark the miscues, or errors, as shown on the chart and model on pages 17 and 18. When the student is finished reading, you should check his or her comprehension by asking the student to tell you about the selection. Make notes on the running record form.

After the running record activity is completed, you will be able to review it and note the student's reading strategies and miscue patterns. This information can be very valuable in planning and reading instruction and determining how the student is developing as a strategic reader.

“How do I KEEP TRACK of what children are learning?”

Marking Oral Reading Miscues

READING MISCUE	MARKING
1. omissions	Circle the word, word part, or phrase omitted. I will let you (go) in.
2. insertions	Insert a caret (∧), and write in the inserted word or phrase. We bought a ∧ parrot. *(big)*
3. substitutions	Write the word or phrase the student substitutes over the word or phrase in the text. Dad fixed ~~my~~ bike. *(the)*
4. mispronunciations	Write the phonetic mispronunciation over the word. Have you ~~fed~~ the dog? *(feed)*
5. self-corrections	Write the letters *SC* next to the miscue that is self-corrected. We took our ~~space~~. *(spot SC)*
6. repetitions	Draw a line under any part of the text that is repeated. It is your <u>garden</u> now.
7. punctuation	Circle punctuation missed. Write in any punctuation inserted. "Are you home(?)" said Frank?
8. hesitations	Place vertical lines at places where the student hesitates excessively. Pretend|this is mine.

Name _Jordan_   Date _January 11_

Book _A Place for Nicholas_   Word count _82_

Child's familiarity with the book:

______ read it before   when? ____________

__✔__ introduced to the book, but has not read it

______ did not get a story preview

Nicholas wanted a place.

Not just any place.

He wanted his ⃝own⃝ place.

"You have ~~this~~ *the* house," _Dad_ said.

"But everybody is here," Nicholas said.

"You have ~~this~~ *the* yard," Kelly said.

"But everybody is here," Nicholas said.

"You have this *the* room," Mom said.

"But Jeff is here," Nicholas said.

"I'll make a place for you," Jeff said.

"You? You are too little," Nicholas said.

"Come back ⃝soon⃝. You'll see," Jeff said.

and Nicholas did see.

And now he has his ⃝very⃝ own place.

Work on :
this
the
that
there

Comments: _likes the story; we discussed how_
Nicholas might feel at the end of the story

Total number of errors _8_

Instant Readers™
Running Record

Name _________________________________ Date _____________________

Book _________________________________ Word count _______________

Child's familiarity with the book:

_______ read it before   when? ____________

_______ introduced to the book, but has not read it

_______ did not get a story preview

Comments: ____

____

Total number of errors ___________

Kidwatching

Kidwatching is the process of monitoring children's ongoing development as they participate in daily activities. Putting the kidwatching philosophy to work in the classroom involves observation, interaction, and analysis.

To build a viable profile of each child as a learner,

- observe a child working independently.
- observe a child working as a member of a group (such as during shared reading and shared writing activities).
- watch a small group of children in action during center-based activities.
- interact with a child during brief encounters or "teachable" moments and during conferences about work in progress.

Remember that

- your questions help both you and the child discover what the child knows.
- a dialogue about a story, drawing, or a favorite book, or a dialogue during center activities yields excellent information about how well a child is using his or her emergent literacy.

Jot down impressions on self-stick notes, index cards, or adhesive labels. Put these in a child's folder or portfolio, or in your own records. Look at several observations made over time, watching for patterns. This information will help confirm what you may already know intuitively about the children.

Anecdotal Records

Anecdotal records are a strategy for capturing and documenting a child's literacy development over time. Anecdotes are brief dated notes about observations made as the child reads, writes, works in centers, or engages in conversations and discussions, or collaboratively works with other children. These observations, recorded as soon as possible after the occurrence, are specific to what the child can do and is doing.

A spiral-bound notebook with several pages set aside for each child in the class can provide a system for collecting anecdotal records. Write phrases or quick notes, with the child's initials, on self-stick notes, index cards, or adhesive labels as you make observations. At the end of the day, transfer the notes, cards, or labels to the appropriate child's page in the notebook.

As you take notes,
- focus on strengths.
- record actions, not reactions. Keep notes objective, nonemotional and nonjudgmental.

- limit what you will try to observe and take notes about. Select two to three behaviors or understandings to focus and collect notes on in a single week.
- include the context surrounding the event. Is it center time? Shared reading?
- remember to take notes about all children, not just the ones who stand out.
- keep fact and interpretation separate.

Anecdotal records are one way to note progress in various contexts and can be useful for conferences with children, parents, or administrators. More significantly, anecdotal records that reflect children's ability, or inability, to use certain skills provide you with direction when making instructional decisions.

Emergent Reading/Writing Checklist

Name____

OBSERVED BEHAVIORS AND STRATEGIES	COMMENTS	DATE
THE EMERGENT READER:		
Enjoys participating in the reading of stories, rhymes, and poems		
Knows where to begin reading the text		
Locates print on the page		
Knows how to track print from left to right and returns to the next line		
Can point out specific words		
THE EARLY READER:		
Recognizes high-frequency words		
Rereads books and shares books with others		
Participates in shared reading and writing		
Expects to get meaning from text		
Uses context clues		
Notices and uses picture clues to predict text		
Sounds out words and letters in reading and writing		
THE FLUENT READER:		
Recognizes known words or word parts in new words		
Retells stories using sequence		
Recalls story words and uses them in writing		
Explores and reads books from other genres		
Monitors and checks reading		
Handles reading/writing challenges		
Reads independently		
Writes independently		
Is confident in him/herself as a reader and writer		

"Now that children *have read* the story, what do I do NEXT?"

POST-READING: LITERACY EXPLORATIONS AND DISCOVERIES

Emerging readers can and should engage in all kinds of meaningful activities after they have read a story. An activity can be as simple as retelling the story to a classmate. Literacy enrichment may include writing, returning to the text to examine language syntax and to master words, and exploring new texts to reinforce learning and expand knowledge about a topic.

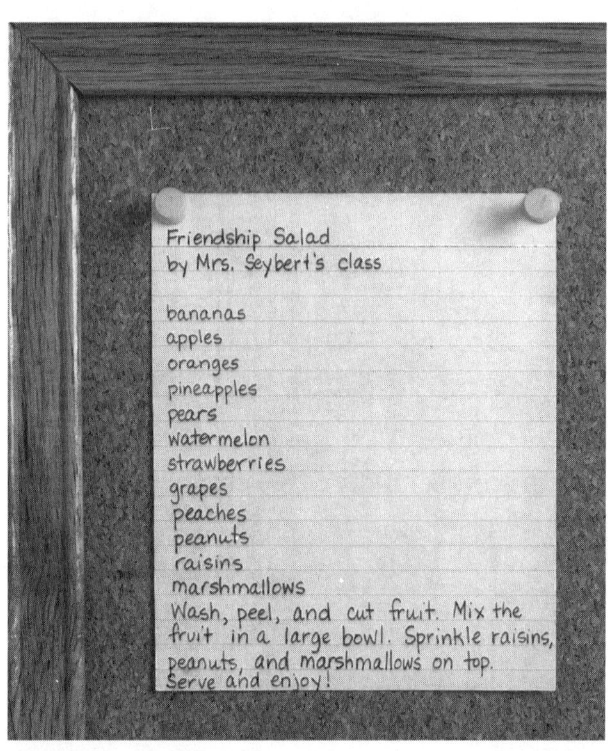

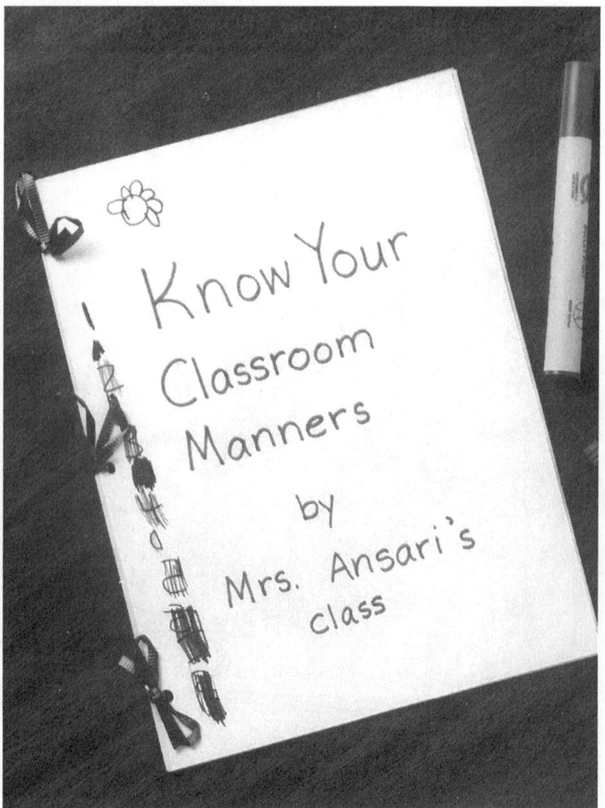

WRITTEN RESPONSES

Several kinds of written responses can be used in the classroom. With a **dialogue journal**, teachers and children can respond together to stories, story characters, and topics. **Shared writing** can be done with a small group or the whole class. **Stories**, **messages**, **letters**, **lists**, **poems**, and **riddles** can be produced collectively with this kind of written interaction. **Story innovations** give children an opportunity to add their own creative spin to a well-liked text. The innovation can be as simple as replacing one word.

As children write or dictate, teachers have a prime opportunity to observe how children use language, apply phonemic awareness to reading and writing, and comprehend text. See more ideas in "Spring into Writing with *Instant Readers*," page 28.

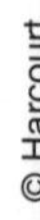

TEXT ANALYSIS

Whether or not teachers have targeted specific phonic or vocabulary instruction for stories, they should incorporate familiar and new story words into study and analysis. With magnetic letters, letter cards, a small chalkboard, or a dry-erase board, children can produce words and work with them. **Word families**, **vowel spellings**, **beginning** and **final letters**, and **base words** can be easily manipulated with these materials. To emphasize **sound-letter correspondences**, help children carefully and accurately pronounce the words.

Point out the following to children:

- similarities in word spellings
- similarities in letter sounds

Moving children to text fluency may involve using **sentence** or **phrase frames**, such as the ones shown on the right.

Other ideas include having children

- write story phrases and sentences on strips of paper, cut out individual words, and then reassemble the strips.
- reread a sentence so it sounds like "talking."
- listen to you reread a sentence.
- write a favorite story sentence in a Reading Log.

A slip-strip like this one allows children to explore new words.

Activities that center around word, phrase, and sentence manipulation provide a window into children's phonemic awareness and knowledge of language syntax.

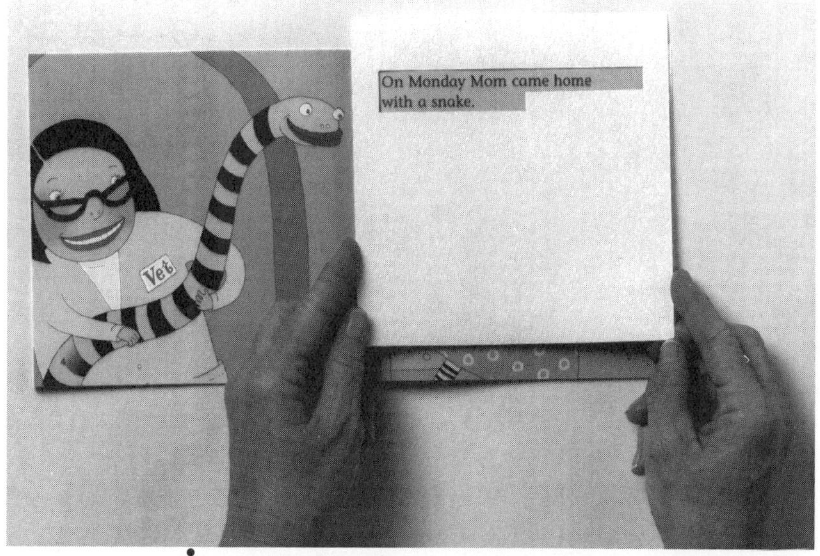

Using a text frame with a book helps children focus on the text.

Post-reading activities complete the story experience with discussions, retellings, analysis of content—all of which return the reader to the text.

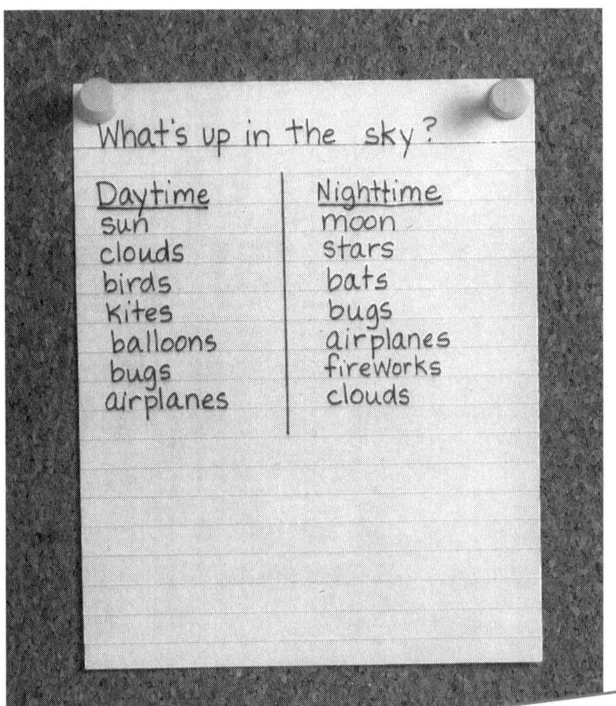

COMPREHENSION AND FLUENCY

The story "talk" begun by teachers and children during pre-reading should be expanded upon after the text has been read. Children may be expected to participate in discussions about the

- story characters and their motivations.
- story setting and plot development.
- genre.
- information provided in nonfiction texts.
- message or moral contained in the story.
- author's and illustrator's craft.
- tone and emotion of the book.

Discussions may be directed by children's responses to a story (such as a much-loved character or a silly rhyme) or chosen by the teacher to assess children's understanding of the story.

Consider having children create and challenge each other with some of the following comprehension activities:

- writing **cloze sentences** about a story
- making and **sequencing story pictures**, **events**, or **sentences**
- **retelling a story** with a Readers Theatre
- **reading stories** to kindergartners or preschoolers
- drawing a mural to **categorize facts** or **information** learned from a story

EXPLORING NEW TEXTS

As teachers develop insights into each child's knowledge about text, it becomes easier to provide appropriate texts that will reinforce learning and stimulate interest in other topics. With the understanding and application of essential reading and writing strategies, children can open the door to further literacy exploration.

For additional information about choosing appropriate books, refer to Dr. Barbara Peterson's article on page 6 and to the additional reading list on page 42.

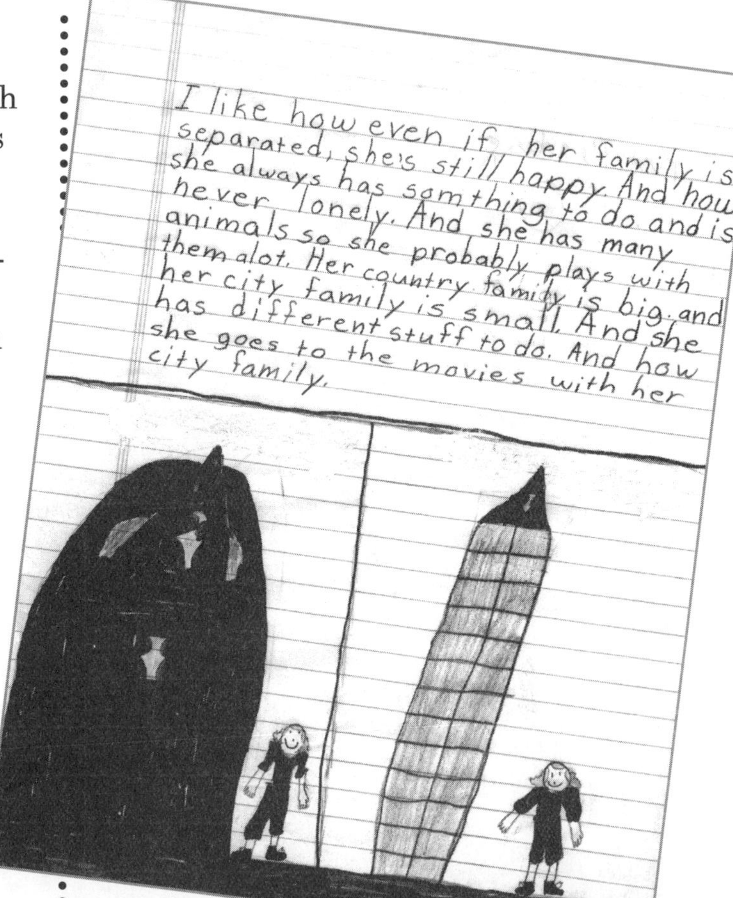

Spring into Writing with *Instant Readers*

by **Dr. Barbara Peterson**

Dr. Peterson is the librarian at Tully Elementary Accelerated Magnet School in Tucson, Arizona.

Writing is an essential component of any early literacy program, even though some students may be able to write only a few letters of their names. Teachers who want their students to progress quickly in reading will provide for many kinds of writing across the curriculum. Reading and writing are reciprocal processes, and writing allows students to

- learn to transfer their thoughts to written form.
- learn to compose and organize their thoughts in a logical form.
- explore relationships between sounds and letters.
- learn about conventions of writing, such as left to right directionality, spacing between words, capitalization, and punctuation.
- create texts they can reread independently or together with a more proficient reader.

Favorite stories from the *Instant Readers* little books can provide many opportunities for students to write independently and in collaboration with their teacher and classmates. Teachers can

- provide students with a response journal (blank paper stapled between sheets of construction paper works well) for daily independent writing and drawing; students are asked to draw and write about the stories they read, using invented spelling and known words; teachers can also take dictation from students about their pictures.
- notice when a particular story inspires an especially enthusiastic response from students and create a special small-group or whole-class writing project; this kind of project should not be started until students have read a story many times and know it well.

A Place for Nicholas is one story likely to stir up many discussions as children empathize with Nicholas's desire to find a place of his own. Here are some possibilities for a writing extension of this particular story.

MAKE A STORY MAP OF ALL THE PLACES NICHOLAS WAS OFFERED FOR HIS OWN.

- **First,** ask students to name all of the places; make a list on chart paper (students can later check with the book to confirm their responses).
- **Second,** ask students to create pictures of each place (if the entire class is working on the story map, have several students work collaboratively on one picture).
- **Next,** when the pictures are finished, ask students to write captions for the pictures. (The words do not need to follow the pattern of the text of the story. The sentence structure should, however, be one that most students could reread independently or with other readers.)

Have students arrange the pictures in sequence. When the work has been checked by children, print the children's writing clearly and have them match the text to the corresponding illustration.

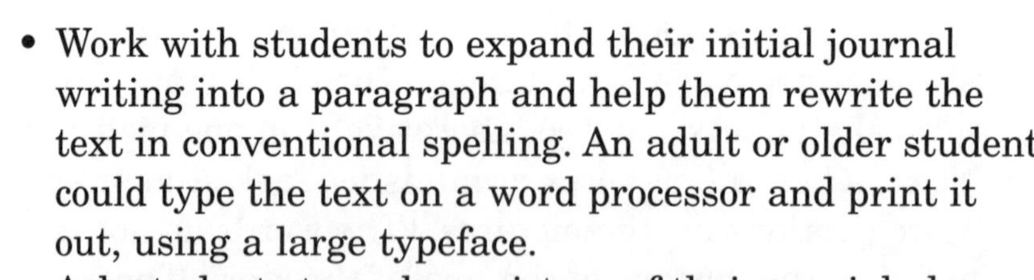

WRITE ABOUT A SPECIAL PLACE.

(This project could begin as independent journal writing.)

- Work with students to expand their initial journal writing into a paragraph and help them rewrite the text in conventional spelling. An adult or older student could type the text on a word processor and print it out, using a large typeface.
- Ask students to make a picture of their special place and put their text under the picture.
- Assemble all the pages to make a class book; ask students to choose a title.
- Use the book for a class text for independent and shared reading.

Other books about special homes could be read. One good example is Michael J. Rosen's *Home*, a collection of writings and illustrations by thirty children's book writers and authors (HarperCollins, 1992).

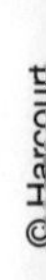

Retell Nicholas's story as a small group or whole class, using a shared (or interactive) writing format.

- Explain to the students that you will all write together to tell the story of what happened to Nicholas.
- Begin by asking the students how they want to begin the story; talking is an important part of the composing process, so encourage students to try out different ways of telling what happened.
- When the group is close to agreement about the first sentence, begin to slowly write the text on the chart paper.
- After writing each word, use a pointer and ask the students to read what they have written so far.
- As the text continues to develop, ask students to do some of the printing.
- During the writing, selectively choose to teach about spacing, capitalization, spelling patterns, or other conventions of print.
- Display the story and encourage children to reread it on their own.

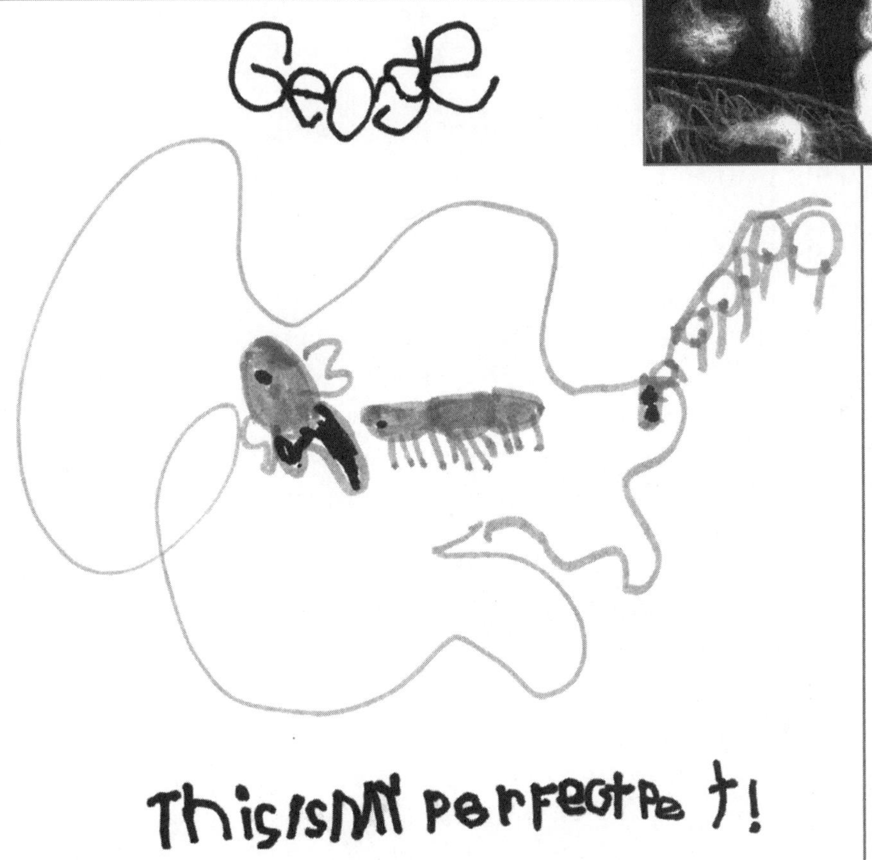

Organized by Level

Instant Readers

Level*	Book Title
1–2	All Fall Down
1–2	The Baby
1–2	Butterflies
1–2	Garden Birthday
1–2	My Dog
1–2	Old MacDonald's Fun Time Farm
1–2	What a Shower!
2–3	Good-Bye, Fox
2–3	Just Like You!
2–3	My Sister Is My Friend
2–3	Spring Pops Up
2–3	The Perfect Pet
2–3	What Could It Be?
2–3	Where Babies Play
3–4	Bird's Bad Day
3–4	Friendship Salad
3–4	"Help!" Said Jed
3–4	My Family Band
3–4	One More Time
3–4	Play Ball!
3–4	What Time Is It?
5–6	After Goldilocks
5–6	Know Your Birthday Manners
6–7	One Little Slip
7–8	Famous Feet
7–8	Today Is Monday
7–8	What Is in the Box?

** Books leveled according to Barbara Peterson's "Profiles of Books for Beginning Readers," page 9 of this publication.*

Organized by Level

Instant Readers

Level*	Book Title
8–9	All I Did
8–9	Four Very Big Beans
8–9	Look What I Can Read!
8–9	Pet Day
8–10	Every Cat
9–10	The Drum
9–10	Frog's Day
9–10	The King Who Loved to Dance
9–10	The Little Chicks Sing
9–10	Lost and Found
9–10	My Wild Woolly
9–10	The Night Walk
9–10	A Place for Nicholas
9–10	Rabbit and Turtle Go to School
9–10	What's Up?
9–11	Let's Visit the Moon
10–11	The Green Grass Grows All Around
10–11	I Was Just About to Go to Bed
10–11	Red
11–12	Alien Vacation
11–12	Green, Green, Green
11–12	Dancing
12–13	Slowpoke Snail
12–14	Pet Jokes and Riddles with Franny and Frank

** Books leveled according to Barbara Peterson's "Profiles of Books for Beginning Readers," page 9 of this publication.*

Organized by Level

Instant Readers

Level*	Book Title
13–14	Davy Crockett and the Wild Cat
13–14	Dream Around the World
13–14	Henry
13–14	How 100 Dandelions Grew
13–14	If You Were a Bat
13–14	A World of Fun
13–14	Plenty of Pets
13–14	What a Catch!
14–15	All Kinds of Rocks
14–15	I Have Another Language
14–15	My Big Surprise
14–15	Secret Show and Tell
14–15	You'll Roar
16–17	Country Family, City Family
16–17	Grandma J
16–17	The Missing Pet Mystery
16–17	Trickster
17–18	Get Ready to Race
17–18	Hiding in Plain Sight
18–19	Buddies
18–19	Molly's Hard Bargain
19–20	One Quiet Afternoon
19–20	White Crow
19–20	Wolf Talk
20+	The Fox and the Crow
20+	How Moon Tricked the Sun
20+	Pretend You're a Tiger

** Books leveled according to Barbara Peterson's "Profiles of Books for Beginning Readers," page 9 of this publication.*

Science Instant Readers

Level	Book Title
1	Animals
1	The Garden
2	Living or Nonliving?
2	My Earth
2	See the Seasons
3	The House Book
4	Animal Homes
4	Water Changes
5	What Do You See?
6	Sink or Float?
7	Rocks
7	What Is a Food Chain?
8	Check the Weather
8	Do Animals Live in Plants?
8	Water's Journey
9	Heat Changes Things
9	Push It or Pull It?
10	Seasons
11	How Does a Plant Grow?
11	Jeff's Magnet
11	Reuse and Recycle

Organized by Level

Science Instant Readers

Level	Book Title
13	Body Parts Work Together
16	Changes Around Us
16	The Fossil Hunters
16	Motion
16	Solids, Liquids, and Gases
16	Water at Work
18	How Does Sound Travel?
18	The Moon
18	The Water Cycle

Level	Book Title	Level	Book Title
9–10	A Place for Nicholas	17–18	Hiding in Plain Sight
13–14	A World of Fun	13–14	How 100 Dandelions Grew
5–6	After Goldilocks	11	How Does a Plant Grow?
11–12	Alien Vacation	18	How Does Sound Travel?
1–2	All Fall Down	20+	How Moon Tricked the Sun
8–9	All I Did	14–15	I Have Another Language
14–15	All Kinds of Rocks	10–11	I Was Just About to Go to Bed
4	Animal Homes	13–14	If You Were a Bat
1	Animals	11	Jeff's Magnet
3–4	Bird's Bad Day	2–3	Just Like You!
13	Body Parts Work Together	5–6	Know Your Birthday Manners
18–19	Buddies	9–11	Let's Visit the Moon
1–2	Butterflies	2	Living or Nonliving?
16	Changes Around Us	8–9	Look What I Can Read!
16–17	Country Family, City Family	9–10	Lost and Found
11–12	Dancing	18–19	Molly's Hard Bargain
13–14	Davy Crockett and the Wild Cat	16	Motion
8	Do Animals Live in Plants?	14–15	My Big Surprise
13–14	Dream Around the World	1–2	My Dog
8–10	Every Cat	2	My Earth
7–8	Famous Feet	3–4	My Family Band
8–9	Four Very Big Beans	2–3	My Sister Is My Friend
3–4	Friendship Salad	9–10	My Wild Woolly
9–10	Frog's Day	1–2	Old MacDonald's Fun Time Farm
1–2	Garden Birthday	6–7	One Little Slip
17–18	Get Ready to Race	3–4	One More Time
2–3	Good-Bye, Fox	19–20	One Quiet Afternoon
16–17	Grandma J	8–9	Pet Day
11–12	Green, Green, Green	12–14	Pet Jokes and Riddles with Franny and Frank
3–4	"Help!" Said Jed		
9	Heat Changes Things		
13–14	Henry		

Organized by Title

Level	Book Title	Level	Book Title
3–4	Play Ball!	4	Water Changes
13–14	Plenty of Pets	8	Water's Journey
20+	Pretend You're a Tiger	13–14	What a Catch!
9	Push It or Pull It?	1–2	What a Shower!
9–10	Rabbit and Turtle Go to School	2–3	What Could It Be?
10–11	Red	5	What Do You See?
11	Reuse and Recycle	7–8	What Is in the Box?
7	Rocks	3–4	What Time Is It?
10	Seasons	9–10	What's Up?
14–15	Secret Show and Tell	2–3	Where Babies Play
2	See the Seasons	19–20	White Crow
6	Sink or Float?	19–20	Wolf Talk
12–13	Slowpoke Snail	14–15	You'll Roar
16	Solids, Liquids, and Gases		
2–3	Spring Pops Up		
1–2	The Baby		
9–10	The Drum		
16	The Fossil Hunters		
20+	The Fox and the Crow		
1	The Garden		
10–11	The Green Grass Grows All Around		
3	The House Book		
9–10	The King Who Loved to Dance		
9–10	The Little Chicks Sing		
16–17	The Missing Pet Mystery		
18	The Moon		
9–10	The Night Walk		
2–3	The Perfect Pet		
18	The Water Cycle		
7–8	Today Is Monday		
16–17	Trickster		
16	Water at Work		

Additional Reading for Emerging Readers

Books to Develop Print Awareness

1 Hunter by Pat Hutchins. Greenwillow, 1982.

26 Letters and 99 Cents by Tana Hoban. William Morrow, 1995.

Cat on the Mat by Brian Wildsmith. Oxford University Press, 1982.

Do You Want to Be My Friend? by Eric Carle. HarperCollins, 1971.

Freight Train by Donald Crews. William Morrow, 1992.

Have You Seen My Duckling? by Nancy Tafuri. Puffin, 1986.

I Read Signs by Tana Hoban. Greenwillow, 1983.

Of Colors and Things by Tana Hoban. Greenwillow, 1989.

Truck by Donald Crews. Mulberry, 1995.

Books for Emerging Readers

Apples and Pumpkins by Anne Rockwell. Simon & Schuster, 1989.

Big Fat Hen by Keith Baker. Harcourt Brace, 1994.

Bread, Bread, Bread by Ann Morris. Lothrop, Lee & Shepard, 1989.

Brown Bear, Brown Bear, What Do You See? by Bill Martin Jr. Henry Holt, 1983.

It Looked Like Spilt Milk by Charles Shaw. HarperCollins, 1947.

Itchy, Itchy Chicken Pox by Grace Maccarone. Scholastic, 1992.

The Jacket I Wear in the Snow by Shirley Neitzel. William Morrow, 1994.

The Missing Tarts by B. G. Hennessy. Puffin, 1991.

One Monday Morning by Uri Shulevitz. Simon & Schuster, 1974.

Silly Willy by Maryann Cocca-Leffler. Grosset & Dunlap, 1995.

Ten Black Dots by Donald Crews. Mulberry, 1995.

Ten, Nine, Eight by Molly Bang. Greenwillow, 1983.

Too Much by Dorothy Stott. Viking Penguin, 1990.

What Will the Weather Be Like Today? by Paul Rogers. Greenwillow, 1990.

Who Is Tapping at My Window? by A. G. Deming. Dutton, 1988.

Whose Mouse Are You? by Robert Kraus. Macmillan, 1970.

BOOKS FOR EARLY READERS

Across the Stream by Mirra Ginsburg.
Greenwillow, 1982.

The Carrot Seed by Ruth Krauss.
HarperCollins, 1945.

Dinosaurs, Dinosaurs by Byron Barton.
HarperCollins, 1989.

Hide and Snake by Keith Baker.
Harcourt Brace, 1991.

Lunch by Denise Fleming. Henry Holt, 1992.

"Pardon?" Said the Giraffe by Colin West.
HarperCollins, 1986.

Peanut Butter and Jelly by Nadine Bernard
Westcott. Dutton, 1987.

Pigs Aplenty, Pigs Galore by David McPhail.
Dutton, 1993.

Quick as a Cricket by Audrey Wood.
Child's Play, 1982.

Walking Through the Jungle by Julie Lacome.
Candlewick, 1993.

What Do You Like? by Michael Grejniec.
North-South, 1992.

The Wind Blew by Pat Hutchins.
Simon & Schuster, 1974.

BOOKS FOR BUILDING INDEPENDENCE

Cookie's Week by Cindy Ward. Putnam, 1988.

Dancing Feet by Charlotte Agell.
Harcourt Brace, 1994.

Fix-It by David McPhail. Dutton, 1987.

Goodnight Moon by Margaret Wise Brown.
HarperCollins, 1974.

Green Eggs and Ham by Dr. Seuss.
Random House, 1960.

Hattie and the Fox by Mem Fox. Bradbury, 1987.

My Brown Bear Barney by Dorothy Butler.
Greenwillow, 1989.

The Napping House by Audrey Wood.
Harcourt Brace, 1984.

Planting a Rainbow by Lois Ehlert.
Harcourt Brace, 1987.

The Very Busy Spider by Eric Carle.
Philomel, 1987.

Who Says Moo? by Ruth Young. Viking, 1994.

BOOKS FOR FLUENT READERS

The Cat in the Hat by Dr. Seuss.
Random House, 1967.

Clifford the Big Red Dog by Norman Bridwell.
Scholastic, 1985.

Frog and Toad Are Friends by Arnold Lobel.
HarperCollins, 1970.

George Shrinks by William Joyce.
HarperCollins, 1985.

Good Books, Good Times selected by Lee Bennett
Hopkins. HarperCollins, 1990.

Good-Night, Owl! by Pat Hutchins. Viking, 1973.

Jump, Frog, Jump! by Robert Kalan.
Greenwillow, 1981.

A Kiss for Little Bear by Else Holmelund
Minarik. HarperCollins, 1968.

On a White Pebble Hill by Chyng Feng Sun.
Houghton Mifflin, 1994.

Surprises selected by Lee Bennett Hopkins.
HarperCollins, 1974.

Three by the Sea by Edward Marshall.
Dial, 1981.

Twist with a Burger, Jitter with a Bug
by Linda Lowery. Houghton Mifflin, 1994.

The Very Busy Spider by Eric Carle.
Philomel, 1984.

The Very Hungry Caterpillar by Eric Carle.
Philomel, 1970.

The Wolf's Chicken Stew by Keiko Kasza.
Putnam, 1987.

Professional Bibliography

E MERGENT LITERACY / INTERVENTION STRATEGIES FOR BEGINNING READERS

Allington, R. & Walmsley, S. (Eds.) (1995). *No Quick Fix.* Columbia University, New York, NY: Teachers College Press.

Butler, A. & Turbill, J. (1987). *Towards a Reading–Writing Classroom.* Portsmouth, NH: Heinemann.

Clay, M. (1991a). Introducing a new storybook to young readers. *The Reading Teacher, 45*(4), 264-273.

Clay, M. (1991b). *Becoming Literate: The Construction of Inner Control.* Portsmouth, NH: Heinemann.

Clay, M. (1993). *Reading Recovery: A Guidebook for Teachers in Training.* Portsmouth, NH: Heinemann.

DeFord, D., Lyons, C. & Pinnell, G. S. (Eds.) (1991). *Bridges to Literacy: Learning from Reading Recovery.* Portsmouth, NH: Heinemann.

Holdaway, D. (1979). *Foundations of Literacy.* New York, NY: Scholastic.

Pinnell, G., Lyons, C., Deford, D., Bryk, A. & Seltzer, M. (1994). Comparing instructional and theoretical models for the literacy education of high risk first graders. *Reading Research Quarterly, 29*(1), 9-39.

Roser, N., Hoffman, J. & Farest, C. (1990). Language, literature, and at-risk children. *The Reading Teacher, 43*(8), 554-559.

Spiegel, D. (1995). A comparison of traditional remedial programs and Reading Recovery: Guidelines for success for all programs. *The Reading Teacher, 49*(2), 86-96.

Strickland, D. & Morrow, L. (Eds.) (1989). *Emerging Literacy: Young Children Learn to Read and Write.* Newark, DE: International Reading Association.

Teale, W. H. & Sulzby, E. (Eds.) (1987). *Emergent Literacy: Reading and Writing.* Norwood, NJ: Ablex.

Wong, S., Groth, L. & O'Flahavan, J. (National Reading Research Center) (1995). Classroom implications of *Reading Recovery®. Reading Today, 13*(3), 12.

Yopp, H. (1992). Developing phonemic awareness in young children. *The Reading Teacher, 45*(9), 696-703.

TEXTS FOR EMERGING READERS

Peterson, B. (1991). Selecting books for beginning readers. In DeFord, D., Lyons, C. & Pinnell, G. S. (Eds.). *Bridges to Literacy: Learning from Reading Recovery.* Columbia University, New York, NY: Teachers College Press.

Clay, M. (1991). Choosing Texts: Contrived Texts, Story Book Texts and Transitional Texts. *In Becoming Literate: The Construction of Inner Control.* Portsmouth, NH: Heinemann.

ONGOING ASSESSMENT

Clay, M. (1985). *The Early Detection of Reading Difficulties.* 3rd ed. Portsmouth, NH: Heinemann.

Farr, R. & Tone, B. (1994). *Portfolio and performance-based assessment.* Fort Worth, TX: Harcourt Brace.